Summer Study
Daily Activity Workbook

Written by **Christine Hood**

Illustrations by **Remy Simard**

New York

New York

An Imprint of Sterling Publishing
387 Park Avenue South
New York. NY 10016

ISBN 978-1-4114-6536-7

Distributed in Canada by Sterling Publishing
c/o Canadian Manda Group, 165 Dufferin Street
Toronto, Ontario, Canada M6K 3H6
Distributed in the United Kingdom by GMC Distribution Services
Castle Place, 166 High Street, Lewes, East Sussex, England BN7 1XU
Distributed in Australia by Capricorn Link (Australia) Pty. Ltd.
P.O. Box 704, Windsor, NSW 2756, Australia

For information about custom editions, special sales, and premium and corporate purchases, please
contact Sterling Special Sales at 800-805-5489 or specialsales@sterlingpublishing.com.

Manufactured in Canada
Lot #:
4 6 8 10 9 7 5 3
03/14

www.flashkids.com

Cover design and production by Mada Design, Inc.

HOW MANY ACORNS?

The squirrel has 15 acorns. In each problem it threw out a different number of acorns. Tell how many acorns are left. Write the subtraction problem on the line.

1.

_15_ – _4_ = _11_

2.

___ – ___ = ___

3.

___ – ___ = ___

4.

___ – ___ = ___

5.

___ – ___ = ___

6.

___ – ___ = ___

7.

___ – ___ = ___

8.

___ – ___ = ___

MATCHING MITTENS

Synonyms are words that mean the same thing.
Match each pair of mittens by finding words that are synonyms. Color each pair the same color.

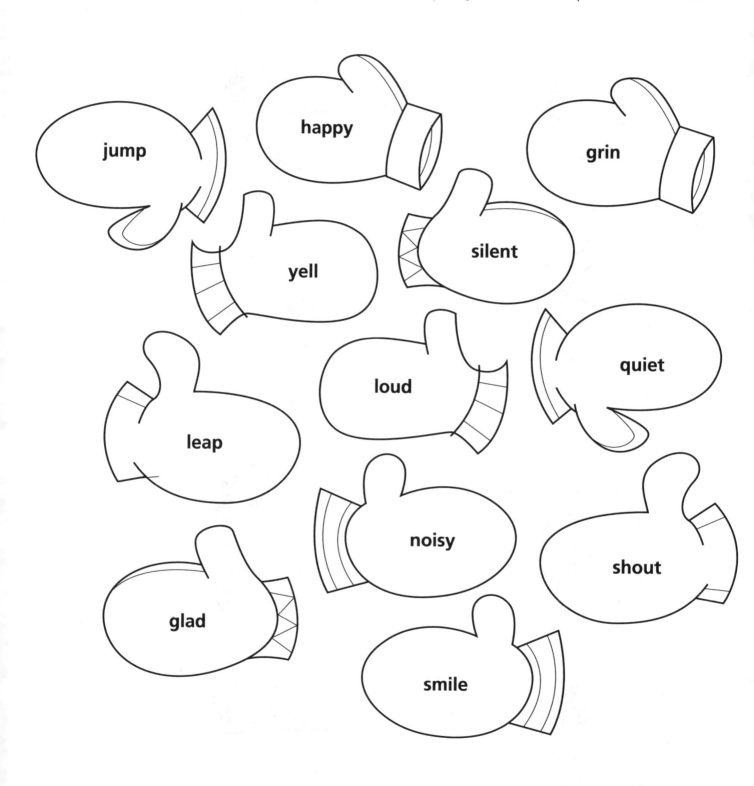

**Day 13:
Synonyms**

BLAST OFF!

Count by fives to connect the dots. Then color the picture.

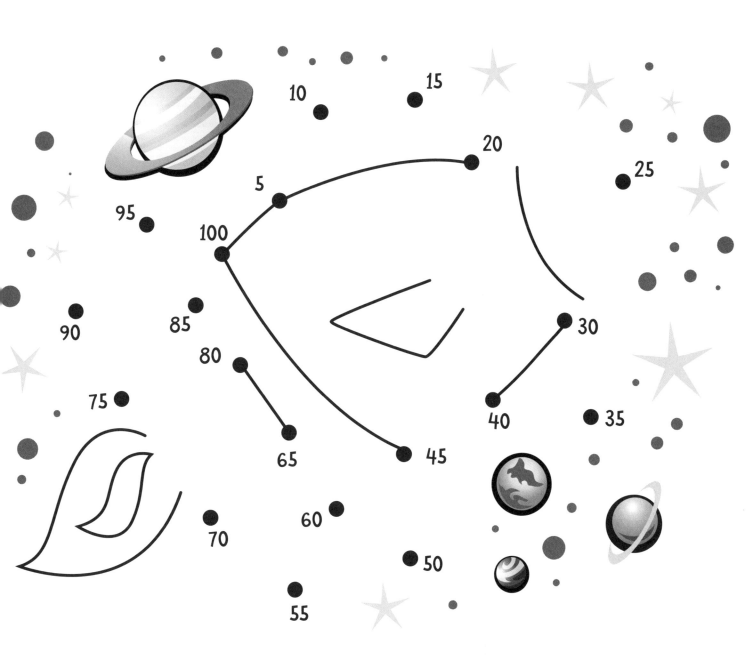

10 15

20

5

25

95

100

90   85   30

80   40   35

75

65   45

60

70

50

55

SPELLING WITH A

Circle the correct spelling of each word. Then find and circle the words in the word search.
Words can go up, down, or diagonal.

1. (today)   tooday   6. waist   wast
2. stain   stane   7. chane   chain
3. playd   played   8. snak   snake
4. awey   away   9. train   trane
5. whale   whalle   10. brayn   brain

E	S	R	U	L	E	S	B	I	P
R	P	L	A	Y	E	D	R	T	L
T	R	C	W	H	E	A	A	L	S
H	A	A	H	A	U	Y	I	O	N
B	Y	T	R	A	I	N	N	S	A
O	I	H	O	Y	I	E	V	T	K
Y	N	E	A	D	H	N	S	A	E
H	E	W	U	D	A	I	I	I	E
N	A	G	O	I	A	Y	A	N	Q
A	E	G	Y	W	H	A	L	E	C

Day 15:
Spelling

COMPARING NUMBERS

Which is more? Which is less? Finish each sentence by writing **more** or **less** in the apple.

1. 15 – 5 is (*less*) than 2 + 9.

2. 10 + 9 is ( ) than 29 – 12.

3. 22 – 10 is ( ) than 9 + 6.

4. 25 + 6 is ( ) than 13 + 19.

5. 33 – 8 is ( ) than 45 – 22.

6. 20 + 20 is ( ) than 15 + 21.

7. 50 – 27 is ( ) than 30 + 11.

8. 62 + 27 is ( ) than 55 + 38.

9. 46 + 17 is ( ) than 28 + 32.

10. 77 – 41 is ( ) than 18 + 27.

11. 86 – 43 is ( ) than 90 – 45.

12. 39 + 16 is ( ) than 23 + 31.

13. 98 – 66 is ( ) than 58 – 28.

14. 39 + 33 is ( ) than 26 + 50.

15. 44 + 19 is ( ) than 31 + 37.

16. 55 – 12 is ( ) than 68 – 27.

**Day 16:
Comparing**

19

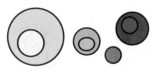

SORTING BOOKS

Help Simon put the books in alphabetical order. Write the titles on the lines.

1.
- Sharks
- Stories
- Snakes
- Shells

Sharks
Shells
Snakes
Stories

2.
- Trees
- Tigers
- Turkey
- Trains

_____
_____
_____
_____

3.
- Magnets
- Money
- Mice
- Moose

_____
_____
_____
_____

4.
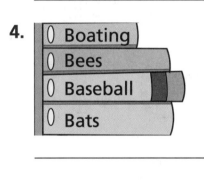
- Boating
- Bees
- Baseball
- Bats

_____
_____
_____
_____

5.
- Holidays
- Horses
- History
- Hats

_____
_____
_____
_____

6.
- China
- Chairs
- Cars
- Clowns

_____
_____
_____
_____

7.
- Soccer
- School
- Spain
- Stars

_____
_____
_____
_____

8.
- Wind
- Whales
- Wishing
- Wigs

_____
_____
_____
_____

9.
- Rhinos
- Rockets
- Roads
- Rice

_____
_____
_____
_____

OUNCES OR POUNDS?

We use **ounces** to measure the weight of light objects. We use **pounds** to measure the weight of heavy objects. Look at each object. Would you use ounces or pounds to weigh it? Circle your answer.

1.

ounces (pounds)

2.

ounces   pounds

3.

ounces   pounds

4.

ounces   pounds

5.

ounces   pounds

6.

ounces   pounds

7.

ounces   pounds

8.

ounces   pounds

9.

ounces   pounds

CREEPY CRAWLY SPIDERS

Read the story. Then answer the questions below.

 Are you scared of spiders? Some people say they are. But most spiders do not bite or harm people. They are very helpful animals. Here are some fun facts about spiders.

- **Spiders are not insects. They are arachnids.**

- **Spiders have eight legs and eight eyes.**

- **Spiders use their sticky webs to catch food. Most spiders eat insects.**

- **Spiders lay their eggs in silk sacs.**

- **Baby spiders are called spiderlings.**

- **Tarantulas are the biggest spiders. They can grow up to 10 inches long!**

- **Tarantulas can eat beetles, frogs, and even birds!**

- **Spiders help people by eating bad insects.**

1. What are spiders?

_____

2. What do most spiders eat?

_____

3. What are baby spiders called?

_____

4. How do spiders help people?

_____

TARGET PRACTICE

Circle the two numbers in each target that add up to the target number.

1.
16
14
12
20

Target: 30

2.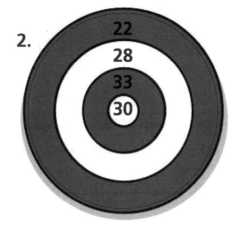
22
28
33
30

Target: 55

3.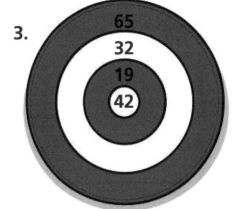
65
32
19
42

Target: 84

4.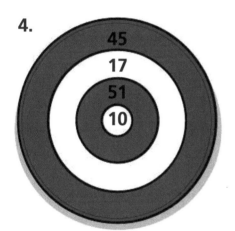
45
17
51
10

Target: 68

5.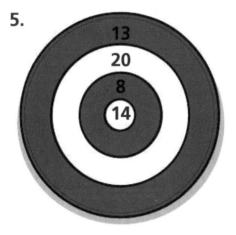
13
20
8
14

Target: 27

6.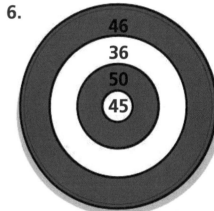
46
36
50
45

Target: 96

7.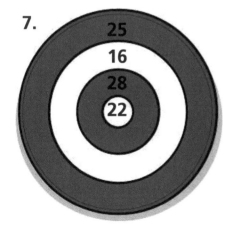
25
16
28
22

Target: 44

8.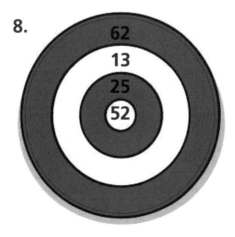
62
13
25
52

Target: 75

9.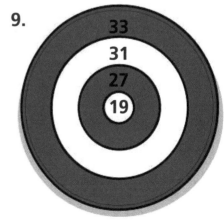
33
31
27
19

Target: 52

**Day 20:
Addition**

23

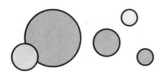

PEN PAL

This letter has a lot of mistakes! Fix the letter by:
- adding capital letters
- adding commas (**,**)
- adding ending punctuation (**. ? !**)

Hint: You should find 22 mistakes.

Example: X̶H̶anna saw pink, white, and silver shells⊙

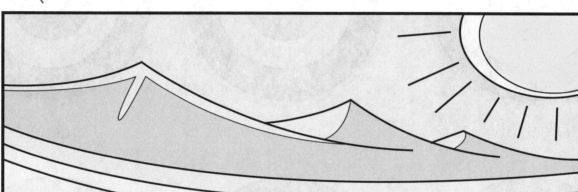

July 10, 2006

Dear kim

i am having a great time at the beach My dogs rex and Lad came too I saw starfish crabs, and fish in the tide pools. Did you know that a starfish can grow a whole new leg

The water here is warm and blue. dad says he will teach me to surf. Isn't that great i can't wait

My sisters Lisa and ana saw a whale today I wish I had seen it too they said the tail was as big as our car. Wow

I hope you are having a great summer i'll see you soon.

your friend

manuel

SOLVE IT!

Solve each problem. Write your answer on the line.

1.

Min saw 18 butterflies.
Nine had purple wings.
How many did not have
purple wings? _____

2.

Ben's quilt has 12 squares.
He has one more quilt just like it.
How many squares are on both
quilts? _____

3.

Jamie has 3 toy cars.
Each car has 4 wheels.
How many wheels are on all 3
cars? _____

4.

Emma has 20 goldfish.
She put 12 in a pond.
How many fish are left in the
bowl? _____

5.

Josh has a bag of 35 candies.
He gave away 15 pieces.
How many pieces are
left? _____

6.

Mina played with 10 kittens.
Half of the kittens were striped.
How many kittens were not
striped? _____

MAKING WORDS

A **compound word** is a word made up of two other words. Draw a line from words on the left to words on the right to make compound words. Then write each new word on the line.

star + fish = starfish

1. snow   card   <u>s</u> n o w f l a k e

2. door   shell

3. sea   cake

4. key   knob

5. bare   lace

6. post   flake

7. shoe   shine

8. pea   foot

9. pan   nut

10. sun   board

Write the circled letters in order to solve the riddle:

What do you call a reptile dessert?

__ __ __ __   __ __ __ __

MATH CROSSWORD

Solve the multiplication problems. Find each answer in the box. Then write it in the puzzle.

| sixteen | three | six | fourteen | eighteen |
| ten | twenty | four | twelve | nine |

1. f o u r t e e n

Across

1. 7 x 2 = _____
4. 2 x 3 = _____
6. 3 x 1 = _____
7. 3 x 3 = _____
8. 4 x 5 = _____

Down

2. 4 x 3 = _____
3. 9 x 2 = _____
4. 4 x 4 = _____
5. 2 x 2 = _____
8. 5 x 2 = _____

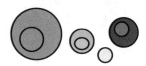 # NOW AND THEN

A **verb** is a word that expresses an action. Circle the verb in each sentence.
Then write the past tense of that verb on the line by adding **-d** or **-ed**.

Past Tense

1. Jason and Cris (play) soccer on the school team.   played

2. Huma bakes cookies for the class.   _____

3. My dogs bark at the mailman.   _____

4. Horses gallop along the beach at sunset.   _____

5. The winds move the leaves across the yard.   _____

6. Shane and Bess want more pizza.   _____

7. Lin and Brett talk on the phone every day.   _____

8. Lots of people visit the new museum.   _____

9. Butter melts on the warm, crispy toast.   _____

10. Tiny ants crawl into the picnic basket.   _____

DIVIDE IT

There are 10 division problems in this puzzle. Circle each problem.

Hints:

Problems can go across or down.

A number can be used in more than one problem.

30	6	5	15	18	20
10	3	25	3	7	4
24	2	12	5	1	5
16	4	4	10	7	2
8	18	3	6	9	14

SPELLING WITH O

Circle the correct spelling in each row.
Then find the circled word that fits in each box and fill in the boxes.

1.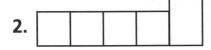

homme	⟨home⟩
boat	boate
clok	clock
snow	snoe
smoke	smocke
sope	soap
throw	thro
rock	roc
drov	drove
roaste	roast

2.

3.

4.

5.

6.

7.

8.

9.

10.

LEAPING LIZARDS

Write the length of each lizard in units. Then change the units to inches.

Units to Inches
4 units = 1 inch
2 units = $\frac{1}{2}$ inch

1.

__12__ units
__3__ inches

2.

_____ units
_____ inches

3.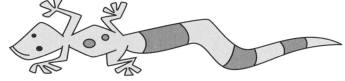

_____ units
_____ inches

4.

_____ units
_____ inches

5.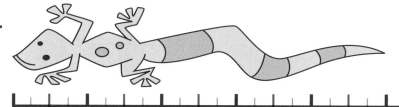

_____ units
_____ inches

6.

_____ units
_____ inches

MAKING CONTRACTIONS

A **contraction** is a word formed by combining two words and leaving out some letters or sounds. For example, "can't" is a contraction of the words "can" and "not."
Write the contraction for each pair of words in ( ). Write it on the line.

1. Dad (can not) take us to the aquarium until Saturday. _can't_

2. (We will) see lots of fish and other sea animals. _____

3. Jess (did not) bring her camera. _____

4. (I am) going to take some pictures for her. _____

5. Sharks (are not) as big as whales. _____

6. Most sharks (do not) hurt people. _____

7. Jess and I (have not) seen real sea otters before! _____

8. A whale (is not) a fish. It is a mammal. _____

9. (Here is) a picture of a blue whale. _____

10. I hope (I will) see a blue whale someday. _____

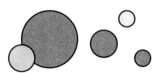

COUNTING TIME

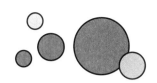

Time Key

1 minute = 60 seconds 1 hour = 60 minutes 1 day = 24 hours 1 week = 7 days
1 year = 12 months

1. Teddy ran the race in 1 minute and 12 seconds. How many seconds did it take?

___72___ seconds

2.  Pine Valley Camp lasts for 28 days. How many weeks does it last?

_____ weeks

3. The movie was 2 hours long. How many minutes was it?

_____ minutes

4.  Earth turns on its axis every 24 hours. How many days is that?

_____ days

5.  Eric walks the dog for 1 hour each day. How many hours does he walk the dog in 2 weeks?

_____ hours

6.  Soccer season lasts 8 weeks. How many days is soccer season?

_____ days

7.  Tess spends $\frac{1}{2}$ of the year in dance lessons. How many months is that?

_____ months

8. Corey reads for 15 minutes each day. How many hours does he read in 8 days?

_____ hours

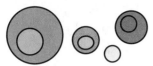

SPELLING WITH I

Circle the correct spelling of each word. Then find and circle the words in the word search.
Words can go up, down, or diagonal.

1. ice   ise
2. lim   lime
3. ti   tie
4. thise   this
5. stir   stur

6. littel   little
7. tiny   tiney
8. spidder   spider
9. circal   circle
10. drive   driv

```
W  I  T  N  O  E  R  B  A  R
E  C  H  U  L  T  A  M  S  I
V  E  Q  C  S  T  I  R  Y  S
S  P  R  A  P  T  E  N  O  J
O  I  H  T  R  D  E  D  Y  S
C  M  Y  L  I  T  T  L  E  I
T  R  A  P  D  N  H  P  S  E
S  I  S  N  O  G  A  I  W  T
E  D  R  I  V  E  D  T  S  I
R  H  I  N  A  J  L  I  M  E
```

FINISH THE PATTERN

Look at each pattern. Finish each pattern by drawing it on the lines.

1.

2.

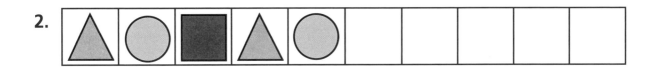

3.

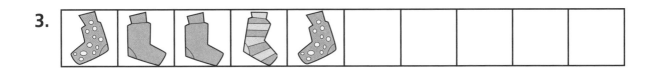

4.

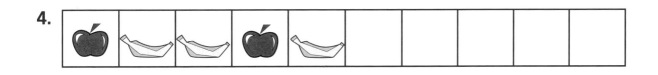

5.

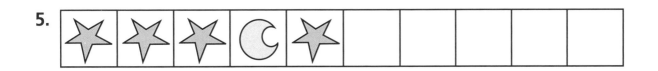

6.

MAGIC SHOES

Read the story. Then answer the questions below.

Meg put on her new red tennis shoes. She tied the laces and looked at herself in the mirror. She knew it right away. These shoes were special.

Meg walked to school with her friend Chad. "I love your shoes," he told her. Meg smiled as she skipped along. It seemed as if she was walking on springs!

At softball practice, Meg almost flew around the bases. Her team was amazed. "I've never seen you run that fast!" her coach cheered. Meg scored three runs.

On her walk home, Meg stopped in her tracks. Her feet were not touching the ground! In fact, she was floating. She was flying!

1. What color are Meg's new shoes? _____

2. What sport does Meg play? _____

3. When did Meg know her shoes were special?

_____

4. What happened to Meg on the way home?

_____

_____

5. On another piece of paper, write a story about what Meg did next.

FLYING FLAGS

Look at the numbers in the flags. Use the Color Key to color the flags.

Color Key

If there is . . .	**Color**
2 in the ones place	**red**
3 in the tens place	**blue**
5 in the hundreds place	**green**
6 in the ones place	**purple**
8 in the tens place	**yellow**

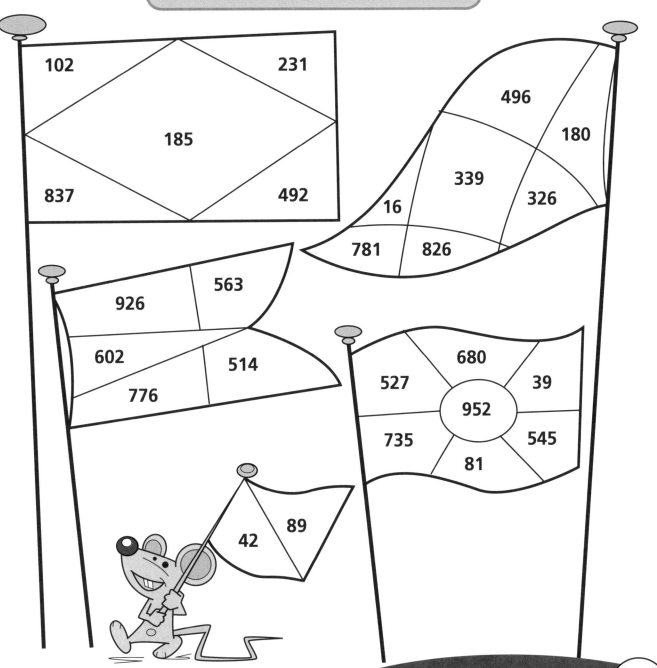

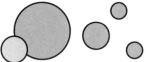
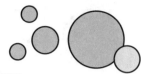

PEN A POEM

You can use adjectives to write a poem! Look at the examples below.

Poem Form:

Noun

2 Adjectives

3 Adjectives

Rename Noun

Example:

Snow

Soft, cold

Fluffy, crunchy, fun

Ice

Write an adjective poem below. Choose an idea from the box or use one of your own.

family	friends	seasons	pets
places	foods	sports	

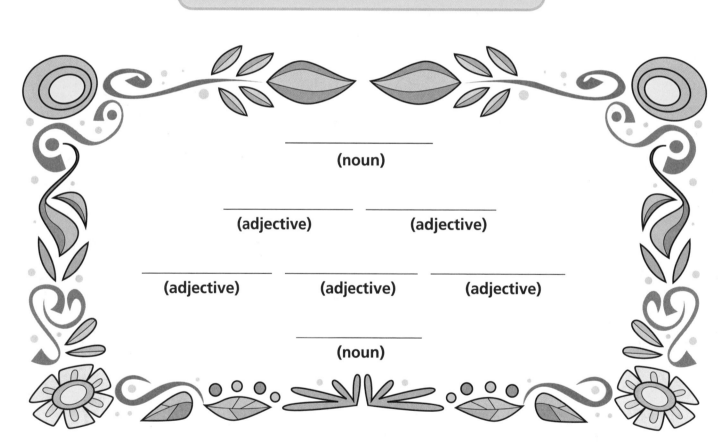

_____

(noun)

_____ _____

(adjective)　　　　　(adjective)

_____ _____ _____

(adjective)　　　(adjective)　　　(adjective)

_____

(noun)

LUNCH ON ME!

Jeff is buying lunch for his friend. Does he have enough money? Circle **YES** or **NO**.

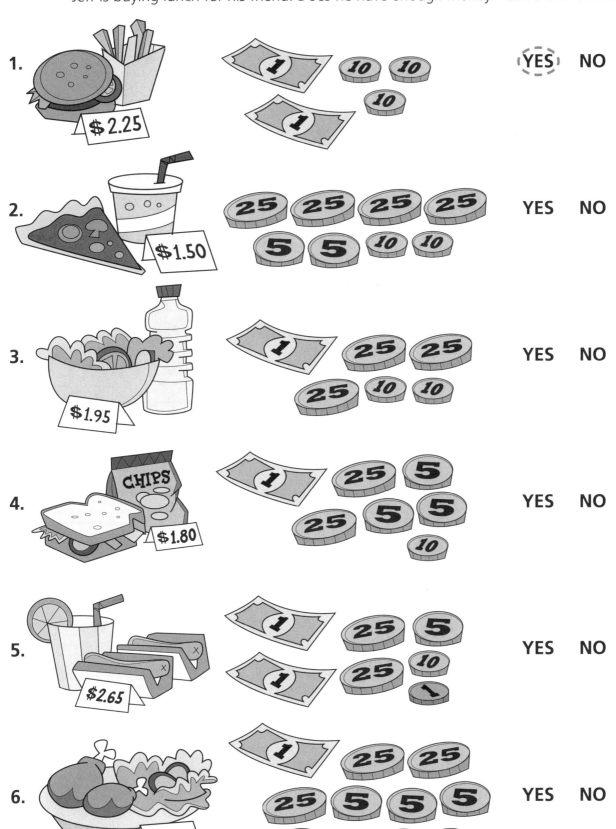

1. $2.25 — (YES) NO

2. $1.50 — YES NO

3. $1.95 — YES NO

4. $1.80 — YES NO

5. $2.65 — YES NO

6. $2.05 — YES NO

PLURALS PLEASE

A **plural** word is one that has more than one thing specified. Add –**s**, –**es**, or –**ies** to each word in ( ) to make it plural. Write the new word on the line to finish each sentence.

1. The zoo has many kinds of _____animals_____ you can visit.   (animal)

2. Mia wishes she could see some _____.   (zebra)

3. I want to see _____ and elephants.   (fox)

4. My _____ and I went to the zoo.   (friend)

5. The reptile house was full of big _____.   (snake)

6. We fed the monkeys _____ of bananas.   (bunch)

7. Lazy lions lay on _____ in the warm sun.   (rock)

8. We got to pet fluffy, white _____.   (bunny)

9. Panda bears peeked at us from behind _____.   (bush)

10. We even saw a tiger playing with her _____.   (baby)

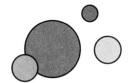

ICE CREAM GRAPH

Read the graph. Then answer the questions.

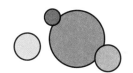

Favorite Ice Cream

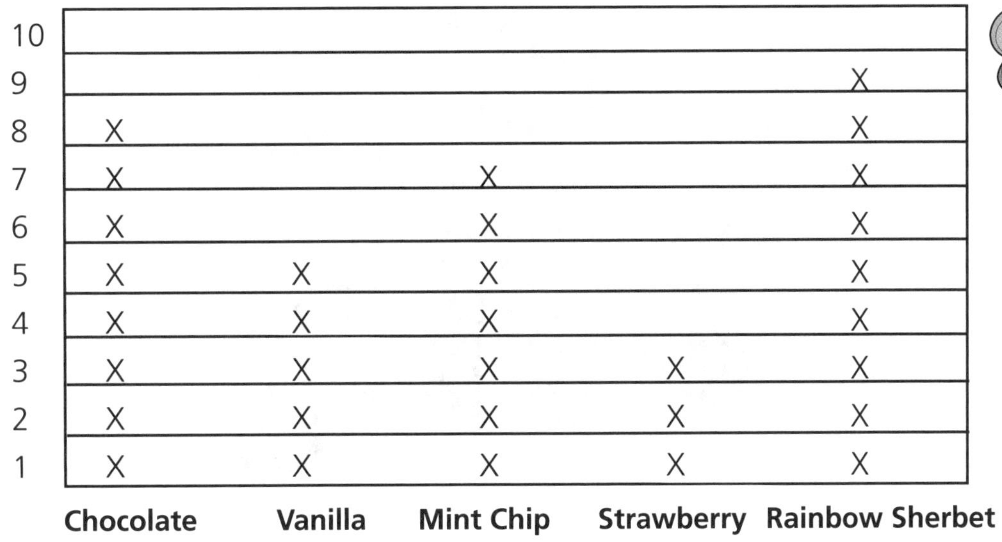

	Chocolate	Vanilla	Mint Chip	Strawberry	Rainbow Sherbet
10					
9					X
8	X				X
7	X		X		X
6	X		X		X
5	X	X	X		X
4	X	X	X		X
3	X	X	X	X	X
2	X	X	X	X	X
1	X	X	X	X	X

1. Which ice cream was the most popular? __rainbow sherbet__

2. What was the second favorite ice cream? _____

3. How many more people liked chocolate than strawberry? _____

4. How many more people liked rainbow sherbet than vanilla? _____

5. How many people are included in the graph all together? _____

6. What is your favorite ice cream? Add your vote to the graph. Then go back and answer each question again. Did any of your answers change? If so, how?

_____

_____

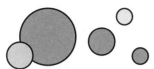
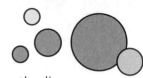

VERB SEARCH

Circle the verb in each sentence. Then write the past tense of that verb on the line.

1. Maya (goes) to the market every Saturday morning. _____**went**_____

2. Carla knows how to play chess. _____

3. Matt breaks track records each school year. _____

4. Peter feels the warm sand between his toes. _____

5. Jon swings the bat better than anyone else. _____

6. The coins sink to the bottom of the well. _____

7. Grandma makes my favorite cookies. _____

8. Todd throws the ball all the way down the field. _____

9. Mr. Jones feeds ducks bread in the park. _____

10. Lan draws pictures of her family. _____

FRACTION FUN

Write the fraction for each picture.

Example:
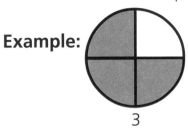

$$\frac{3}{4}$$

1.
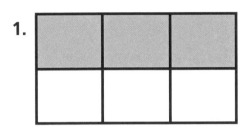

_____

2.
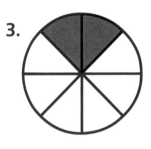

_____

3.
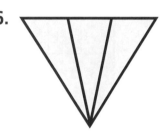

_____

4.
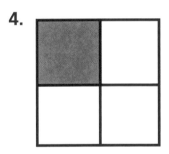

_____

5.
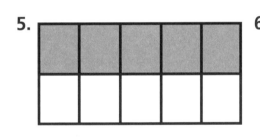

_____

6.
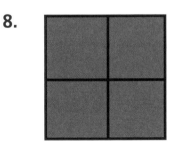

_____

7.
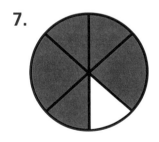

_____

8.

_____

9.
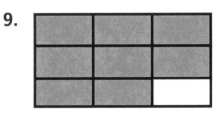

_____

SPELLING WITH E

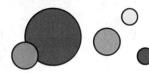

Circle the correct spelling in each row.
Then find the circled word that fits each box and fill in the boxes.

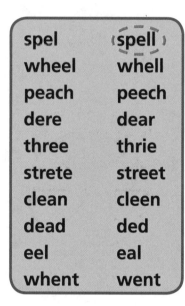

spel	(spell)
wheel	whell
peach	peech
dere	dear
three	thrie
strete	street
clean	cleen
dead	ded
eel	eal
whent	went

1. **s** **p** **e** l l

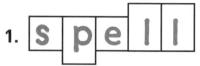

2.

3.

4.

5.

6.

7.

8.

9.

10.

FACES OF MONEY

Write the value for each set of coins. Then write the number word on the lines.

1.  (25) (25) (10) (10)

___70___ ¢

s e v (e) n t y

2.  (10) (10) (5) (10) (5)

_____ ¢

(◯) __ __ __ __

3.  (25) (10) (10) (5) (5)

_____ ¢

__ (◯) __ - __ __ __

4.  (5)  (5) (5) (5) (5) (5) (1)

_____ ¢

__ __ __ __ __ - __ (◯) __

5. (10) (10) (10) (5) (5) (10) (10) (1) (1) (1) (1)

_____ ¢

__ __ __ __ - __ __ (◯) __

6.  (25) (25) (10) (10) (5) (1) (10)

_____ ¢

__ __ __ __ __ -(◯)__ __

7.  (10) (10) (5) (5) (1) (5) (5) (1)

_____ ¢

__(◯)__ __ - __ __ __ __

8.  (25) (25) (25) (5) (5) (5)

_____ ¢

(◯) __ __ __ __

Write the circled letters in order to answer the question:

Which U.S. President's face is shown on the nickel?

J ____ ____ ____ ____ ____ ____ ____ ____

SEARCH FOR SENTENCES

Read each paragraph. Circle the incomplete sentences.

1. Azra planted a flower garden in the spring. Each day she watered the warm earth. First, tiny seedlings. Then buds began to form. Azra knew that soon pink and purple. Soon, big flowers!

2. Did you know there are two kinds of elephants? Are Asian and African. Asian elephants have smaller ears. Have five front toes. African elephants are bigger. Both males and females have tusks. They only have four front toes. Like elephants? I do!

3. Got a snowboard for his birthday. Over the snow really fast! Dave used to ride a skateboard. But he likes the snow better. Rides better and better. He joined a snowboarding club. Now Dave can get into some contests.

4. When I grow up, I want to be an astronaut. It would be fun to fly in space. All the planets. I could count all the stars. I might even see a comet! Trip to the moon. I could gather moon rocks. To my family.

5. Now choose one of these paragraphs. Rewrite it on the lines below. Make sure all the sentences are complete!

_____

_____

_____

_____

_____

STARRY SKY

Multiply. Find each pair of stars with the same product. Color them the same color.

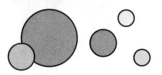
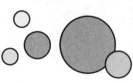

SPORTS STORIES

Read each story. Write the letter of the sport described on the line.
Hint: Not all sports will be used.

| A hiking | B baseball | C tennis | D swimming |
| E biking | F boating | G skiing | |

1. Dina put on her suit. She grabbed a towel and walked to the beach. Before going in, she put on lots of sunscreen. She did not want to get a sunburn.

___D___

2. Trey put on his boots. He put a snack and a bottle of water in his pack. Then he looked at his map. Trey grabbed his walking stick and started up the trail.

_____

3. Luke put on his cap and went outside. He carried his mitt and bat over his arm. He would put on his cleats at the field. It was a perfect day for a game!

_____

4. "Put on your life jacket," Mom said. Krista put it on. Then they pushed off from the dock. Mom and Krista put their oars in the water and started to row.

_____

5. Carlos peddled as fast as he could. His legs were pumping. His hands gripped the handlebars. Wind whistled by his helmet. He made it to the top of the hill!

_____

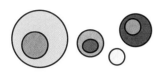
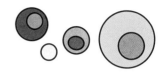

TRAIN TIME

Read the train schedule. Then answer the questions.

Train	To	Departs	Arrives
2	Vast Valley	10:00 AM	12:30 PM
4	Wild Woods	11:15 AM	2:15 PM
6	Teeny Town	12:45 PM	3:30 PM
8	Snow City	2:30 PM	4:45 PM
10	Cat's Creek	5:00 PM	9:15 PM

1. Which train has the shortest trip? _____ Train 8 _____

2. Which train has the longest trip? _____

3. How long is the trip to Teeny Town? _____

4. How much longer is the trip to Wild Woods than to Vast Valley?

_____

5. How much longer is the trip to Cat's Creek than to Snow City?

_____

6. The train to Vast Valley is $1\frac{1}{2}$ hours late. What time will it arrive?

_____

NAME THE SENTENCE

A **telling** sentence makes a statement. It ends with a period. (**.**)
A **command** tells someone to do something. It ends with a period. (**.**)
An **asking** sentence asks a question. It ends with a question mark. (**?**)
An **exclamation** shows strong feeling. It ends with an exclamation point. (**!**)

Add the correct ending punctuation to each sentence. Then write **T** for **telling**, **C** for **command**, **A** for **asking**, and **E** for **exclamation**.

1. Did you see that shooting star? __A__

2. Wow, there are many, many stars in the sky ____

3. Nine planets are in our solar system ____

4. Would you like to go to the moon ____

5. Bring moon rocks back from your trip ____

6. Get ready to ride the fast rocket ____

7. Mars is called the red planet ____

8. Is the sun a planet or a star ____

9. Never look at the sun ____

10. How many rings are around Saturn ____

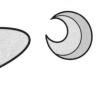

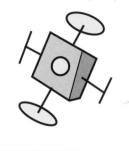

TAKE A GUESS

An **estimate** is a guess. Find each object shown below. Estimate the length of the object in inches. Then use a ruler to check your estimate.

1.

Estimate: A pencil is about _____ inches long.

Measure: A pencil is _____ inches long.

2.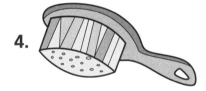

Estimate: My foot is about _____ inches long.

Measure: My foot is _____ inches long.

3.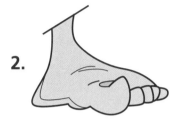

Estimate: A sock is about _____ inches long.

Measure: A sock is _____ inches long.

4.

Estimate: A brush is about _____ inches long.

Measure: A brush is _____ inches long.

5.

Estimate: A notebook is about _____ inches long.

Measure: A notebook is _____ inches long.

6.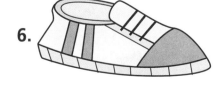

Estimate: A shoe is about _____ inches long.

Measure: A shoe is _____ inches long.

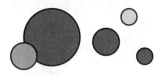
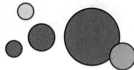

THE MAIN IDEA

The main idea tells what a paragraph is mostly about. Read each paragraph.
Then circle the main idea.

1. Fall is the best time of the year. The air is crisp and cool. I jump in piles of colorful leaves. Mom bakes apple pie. But best of all, I get to go back to school and see my friends.

a) Fall weather is cold.

b) Fall is a great season.

c) I like leaves.

2. Some people think cats can't be trained. This is not true. It's actually very easy! First, be calm and gentle. Repeat tricks over and over again. Give your cat lots of treats as a reward. Soon your kitty will do anything you want.

a) Cats love treats.

b) Cats can't do tricks.

c) You can train your cat.

3. Have you ever been to the circus? Clowns make you laugh. People ride elephants. Acrobats leap through the air. There's so much to see and do. I can't wait to go to the circus!

a) Clowns are funny.

b) The circus is fun.

c) There are elephants at the circus.

4. Be safe when you ride your bike. Wear a helmet to protect your head. Look both ways before crossing the street. Make a signal before turning. Always look out for cars. Drivers may not see you. Have fun, but be safe.

a) Bike safety is important.

b) Drivers never see bikers.

c) Bike helmets are cool.

ANIMAL RIDDLES

Write the answer to each problem in the box. Use the Answer Key to find the letter that matches each answer. Write the letters on the lines below to answer the riddles.

Answer Key

4	7	0	11	2	5	8	1	9	3	10	12	6
A	K	G	S	D	P	U	O	H	R	C	Q	E

What happens when a duck flies upside down?

72 ÷ 8	66 ÷ 11
9	

H   _____

144 ÷ 12	56 ÷ 7	16 ÷ 4	50 ÷ 5	21 ÷ 3	99 ÷ 9

____ ____ ____ ____ ____ ____

64 ÷ 8	60 ÷ 12

____ ____

What do you call a pig who drives?

24 ÷ 8	11 ÷ 11	12 ÷ 3	18 ÷ 9		45 ÷ 5	10 ÷ 10	7 ÷ 0

____ ____ ____ ____   ____ ____ ____

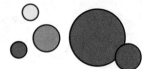

Circle the correct spelling of each word. Then find and circle the words in the word search. Words can go up, down, or diagonal.

1. turtel (turtle)
2. cube   cueb
3. birst   burst
4. push   pushe
5. pupel   pupil

6. tru   true
7. fur   furr
8. funny   funey
9. fuel   fule
10. bluw   blue

```
W   T   R   U   T   B   H   O   A   Y

I   P   U   P   I   L   E   S   R   P

V   A   C   R   U   A   T   L   T   U

B   U   R   S   T   O   R   E   W   S

U   G   H   O   R   L   U   L   P   H

M   L   K   M   Y   N   E   S   L   I

A   K   B   N   O   U   C   H   U   N

U   O   N   L   F   E   A   T   O   R

K   U   L   C   U   B   E   S   U   S

F   I   H   U   P   E   J   F   U   E
```

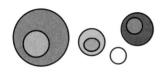

LOTS OF LEGS

Read the questions. Write your answers on the lines.

1. How many legs are on …

2 chicks __4__   3 chicks __6__   4 chicks __8__   5 chicks __10__

2. How many legs are on …

1 horse _____   3 horses _____   6 horses _____   8 horses _____

3. How many legs are on …

3 bugs _____   5 bugs _____   9 bugs _____   11 bugs _____

4. How many legs are on …

2 spiders _____   5 spiders _____   10 spiders _____   12 spiders _____

5. How many arms and legs are on …

2 crabs _____   4 crabs _____   9 crabs _____   12 crabs _____

WHAT HAPPENED NEXT?

Read each paragraph. Then write what happened next on the lines.

1. Big, puffy gray clouds filled the sky. The wind began to blow. As Sam walked home from school, she felt droplets on her face. Leaves blew around her feet in circles. Sam realized she had left her umbrella at home. What happened next?

_____

_____

_____

2.

Ethan was a good pitcher. He and his dad practiced every day after school. The big game was coming up fast. Ethan knew the more he practiced, the better he would be. On the day of the game, Ethan was nervous. He sat on the bench, his heart pounding. What happened next?

_____

_____

_____

3. The earth shook. The huge mountain rumbled as smoke poured from its top. For days, the mountain spoke. It didn't speak softly. It roared! But on this day, it roared louder. Smoke and ash filled the sky. What happened next?

_____

_____

_____

WRITE IT OUT

Write out each number in thousands, hundreds, tens, and ones.

Example: 3,550 = 3,000 + 500 + 50 + 1

1. 8,295

_____ = _____ + _____ + _____ + _____

2. 1,047

_____ = _____ + _____ + _____ + _____

3. 9,962

_____ = _____ + _____ + _____ + _____

4. 6,813

_____ = _____ + _____ + _____ + _____

5. Write as many 3-digit numbers as you can using: 5, 3, 9.

_____   _____   _____

_____   _____   _____

Circle the smallest number. Cross out the largest number.

6. Write as many 3-digit numbers as you can using: 6, 8, 2

_____   _____   _____

_____   _____   _____

Circle the smallest number. Cross out the largest number.

INTERESTING WORDS

Good writing has interesting words. There is usually more than one way to describe something!
Read the words in the word box.

| sticky | irritated | glad | asked | thrilled | angry | gooey | cranky |
| roared | rough | joyful | groaned | cross | prickly | cried | cheerful |

- Find 4 words that mean **happy**.
- Find 4 words that mean **mad**.
- Find 4 words that mean **said**.
- Find 4 words that describe how something **feels** when you touch it.

Write each group of words in the word puzzles.

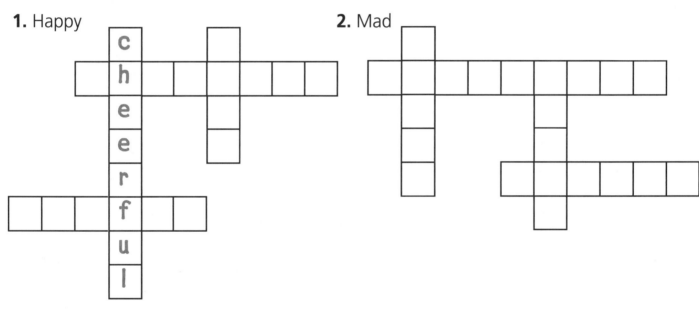

1. Happy

2. Mad

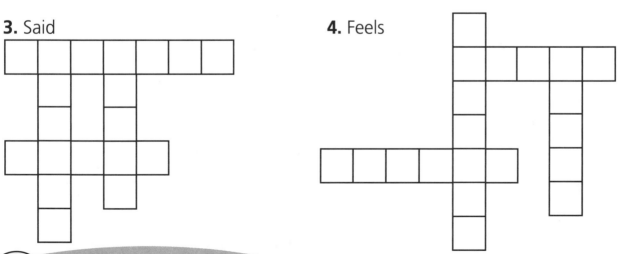

3. Said

4. Feels

OUR PETS

This is a **pie chart**. It shows the number of people who have different kinds of pets.
Read the chart. Then answer the questions.

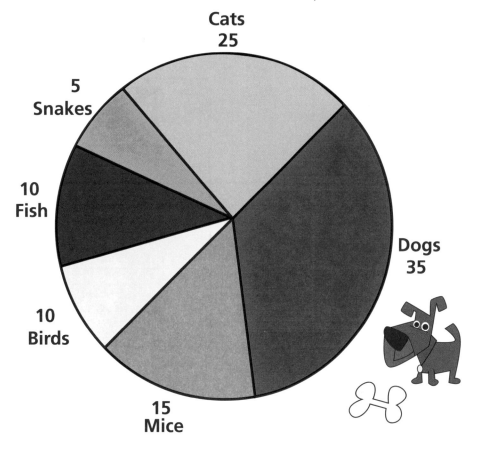

Cats
25

5
Snakes

10
Fish

Dogs
35

10
Birds

15
Mice

1. How many people have dogs? _____

2. How many people have cats? _____

3. How many more people have dogs than fish? _____

4. How many more people have mice than snakes? _____

5. How many people do not have cats? _____

6. How many people have pets all together? _____

SURPRISE IN THE BOX

Think of an object to put in each box. Write five adjectives to describe it in the box.
Then write the name of the object.

1.

It is a _____!

2.

It is a _____!

3.

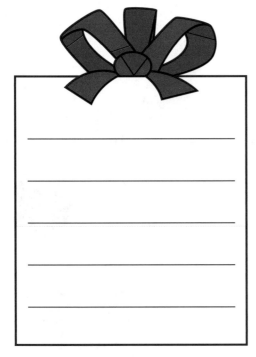

It is a _____!

4.

It is a _____!

# LIQUID MEASURES

Use the Measuring Key to solve the problems. Then write your answers in the crossword puzzle.
Use number words.

Measuring Key

3 teaspoons (tsp.) = 1 tablespoon (Tbs.)

2 Tbs. = 1 ounce

8 ounces = 1 cup

2 cups = 1 pint

2 pints = 1 quart

4 quarts = 1 gallon

Across

2. $\frac{1}{2}$ gallon = _____ cups

4. 12 pints = _____ quarts

5. 6 cups = _____ pints

7. 33 tsp. = _____ Tbs.

9. 1 quart = _____ ounces

Down

1. 2 cups = _____ ounces

3. 3 Tbs. = _____ tsp.

6. 10 cups = _____ ounces

8. 1 quart = _____ cups

10. 32 Tbs. = _____ cups

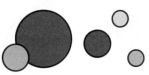

DEAR FRIEND...

Write a letter to a friend or a family member. Tell this person about something special you are doing this summer. Are you taking a special trip? Are you taking lessons? Are you visiting a relative?

Remember to follow these rules:
- **Use interesting words.**
- **Use correct punctuation.**
- **Use complete sentences.**

_____
(Date)

Dear _____,

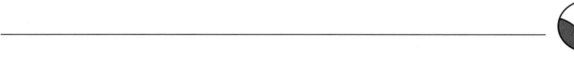

Your friend,

_____

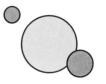

PERIMETER PUZZLERS

Perimeter is the distance all the way around the edge of an object.

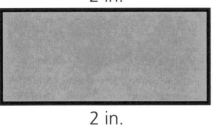

2 in.

4 in.   4 in.

2 in.

P = 2 in. + 2 in. + 4 in. + 4 in. = 12 in.

Write the perimeter of each shape.

1.

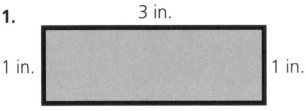

3 in.

1 in.   1 in.

3 in.

P = _____

2.

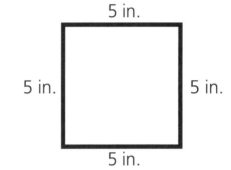

5 in.

5 in.   5 in.

5 in.

P = _____

3.

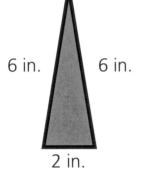

6 in.   6 in.

2 in.

P = _____

4.

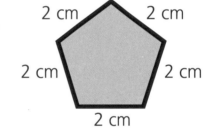

2 cm   2 cm

2 cm   2 cm

2 cm

P = _____

5.

8 in.

4 in.   4 in.

8 in.

P = _____

6.

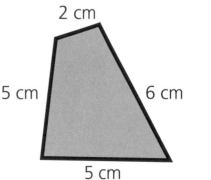

2 cm

5 cm   6 cm

5 cm

P = _____

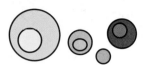

DETAILS, DETAILS!

Every paragraph has a main idea. The main idea is supported by **details**. These details further describe and develop the main idea.

Underline the supporting details in each paragraph.

1. I took my first train ride today. I sat by the window so I could watch the world go by. We crossed over a river. When we passed through the train stations, people waved at me! I waved back with a big smile on my face. What a great trip!

2. Rainbows form when water and light come together. The water can come from anywhere. It can be rain. It can be spray from a garden hose. It can come from a water fountain. The water source is not important.

3. Now, write your own main idea and supporting details. Write your main idea in the center circle. Write details about that idea in the circles around it.

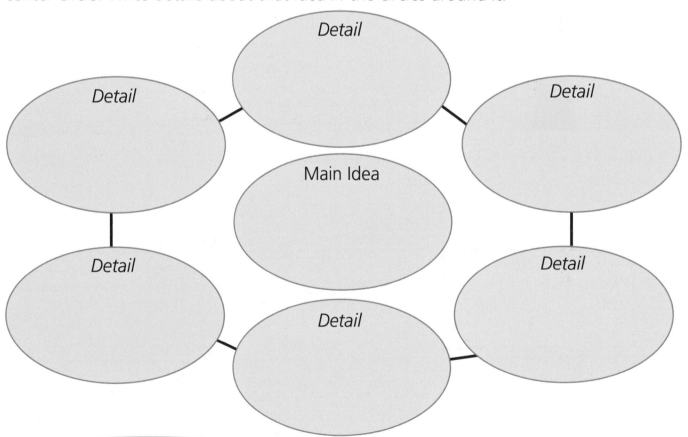

BRAIN STUMPERS

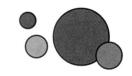

Read the clues to solve each problem.

1. How many marbles are in the bag?
• There are more than 20 and less than 30.
• You can divide the marbles equally into groups of 3.
• If you divide the marbles into groups of 5, 1 will be left over.

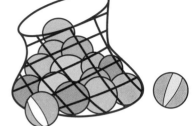

There are __21__ marbles in the bag.

2. Keri, Ana, Ahmad, and Juan were all born the same year. Who is the oldest? Write 1, 2, 3, 4 to put the children in order, oldest to youngest.
• Juan's birthday is between Ahmad's and Keri's.
• Ana has the first birthday in the group.
• Keri is younger than Ahmad.

Keri _____   Ana _____   Ahmad _____   Juan _____

3. How many coins are in the jar?
• There are more than 30 and less than 50.
• You can divide the coins equally into groups of 6.
• If you divide the coins into groups of 5, 3 will be left over.

There are _____ coins in the jar.

READ ALL ABOUT IT!

Newspaper articles tell about events in the community. Look at a newspaper. Read the headlines. They grab your attention! Articles also answer these questions:

Who? What? When? Where? How?

Write an article about an event in your family or neighborhood. Make sure to answer the questions who, what, when, where, and how. Remember to write a great headline!

Draw a picture.

RELAY RACERS

Solve the problems. Color the spaces with answers that are odd numbers.
To solve the riddle, write the letters that appear in the colored spaces on the lines below.

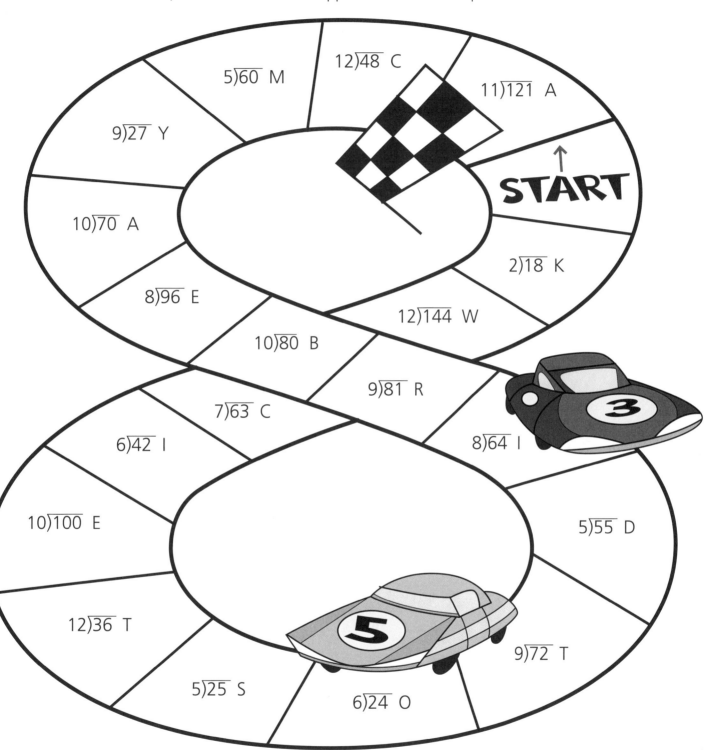

$5\overline{)60}$ M

$12\overline{)48}$ C

$11\overline{)121}$ A

$9\overline{)27}$ Y

START

$10\overline{)70}$ A

$2\overline{)18}$ K

$8\overline{)96}$ E

$12\overline{)144}$ W

$10\overline{)80}$ B

$9\overline{)81}$ R

$7\overline{)63}$ C

$6\overline{)42}$ I

$8\overline{)64}$ I

$10\overline{)100}$ E

$5\overline{)55}$ D

$12\overline{)36}$ T

$9\overline{)72}$ T

$5\overline{)25}$ S

$6\overline{)24}$ O

What has a foot on each side and one in the middle?

___ ___ ___ ___ ___ ___ ___ ___ ___ ___ ___

CHANGING WORDS

A **prefix** is a word part added to the front of a base word. A prefix changes the meaning of that word. Read the meanings of the prefixes. Then read the definitions below. Make a new word to match each definition by adding a prefix. Then write a brand new word with the same prefix.

Prefixes

re- again		**un**- not	
bi- two		**over**- too much	
under- below		**non**- not	
mis- wrong		**multi**- many, much	

New word

1. Write again	___re___ write	reread _____
2. Cycle with two wheels	_____ cycle	_____
3. Not happy	_____ happy	_____
4. Below ground	_____ ground	_____
5. Pay too much	_____ paid	_____
6. Not able	_____ able	_____
7. Many colored	_____ colored	_____
8. Count wrong	_____ count	_____
9. Does not stop	_____ stop	_____
10. Heat again	_____ heat	_____

Write two sentences. Use one of your new words in each sentence.

11. _____

12. _____

WHICH SHAPES?

Look at each set of shapes. Circle the correct answer.

1. Which shape is a cube?

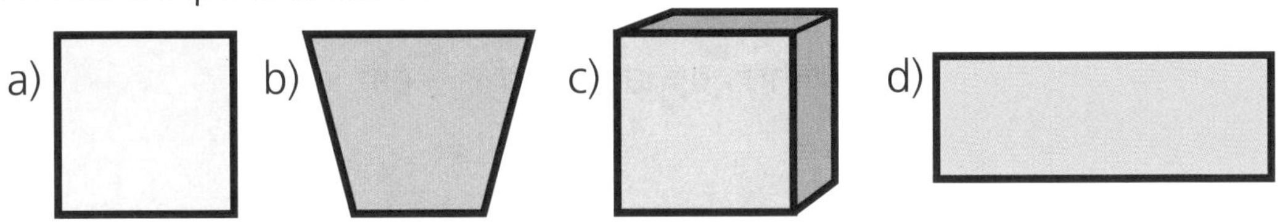

a) b) c) d)

2. Which shape contains two triangles?

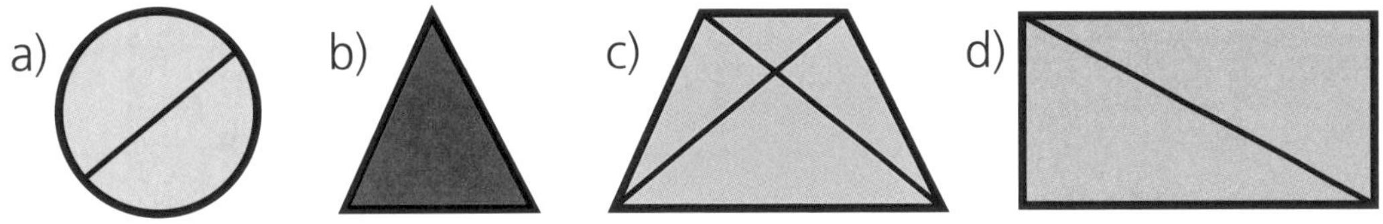

a) b) c) d)

3. Which shape is a cylinder?

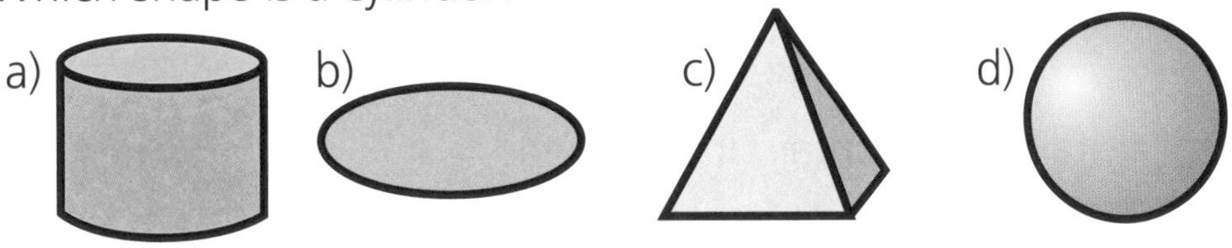

a) b) c) d)

4. Which shape is divided into equal halves?

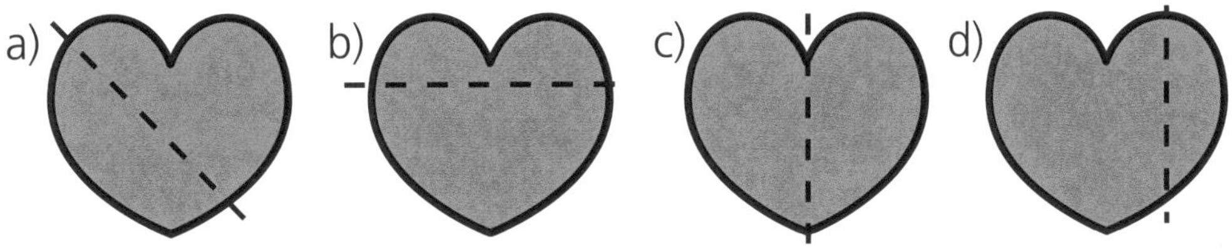

a) b) c) d)

5. Which shape contains two squares?

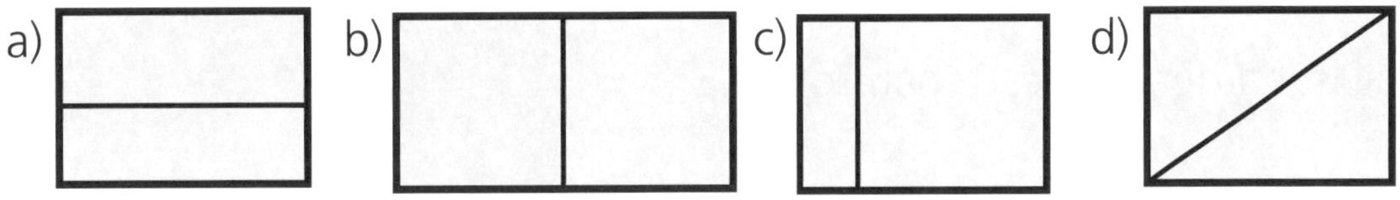

a) b) c) d)

6. Which shape is a sphere?

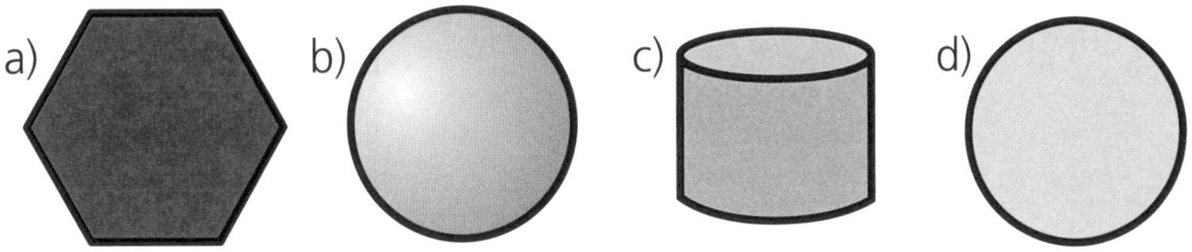

a) b) c) d)

7. On a separate piece of paper, use only circles and triangles to draw a picture of an animal.

MAKING COMPARISONS

Adjectives that compare two things usually end in **–er.**
Example: Chloe is <u>taller</u> than Zane.

Adjectives that compare more than two things usually end in **–est.**
Example: Zane is the <u>smartest</u> boy in class.

Circle the adjective that best completes each sentence.

1. Meg is the (sweeter, (sweetest)) girl in second grade.

2. Whales are the (bigger, biggest) animals in the sea.

3. My speech is 10 minutes (longer, longest) than yours.

4. Mount Everest is the (taller, tallest) mountain in the world.

5. Nick is a (stronger, strongest) ball player than Jared.

6. Cheetahs can run (faster, fastest) than lions.

7. The sun seems (brighter, brightest) today than yesterday.

8. My Grandpa is the (funnier, funniest) man I know.

9. I think football is (harder, hardest) than soccer.

10. February is the (shorter, shortest) month of the year.

Use these adjectives to write sentences that compare.

11. cold _____

12. nice _____

SHOWING FRACTIONS

Divide each shape into the the number of parts shown in the fraction. Then shade in the parts to show the fraction.

1.

$$\frac{5}{8}$$

2.

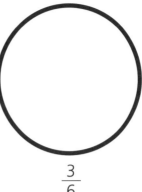

$$\frac{3}{6}$$

3.

$$\frac{4}{4}$$

4.

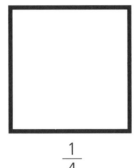

$$\frac{1}{4}$$

5.

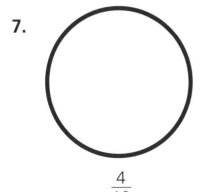

$$\frac{1}{2}$$

6.

$$\frac{8}{12}$$

7.

$$\frac{4}{10}$$

8.

$$\frac{2}{8}$$

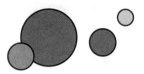
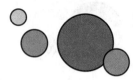

WHERE ARE YOU?

Use the clues to find the answers. Write your answers in the puzzle.

starfish   beach   shells   ocean   sand   sunscreen
fire   touch   salty   stories   roast

Do you want to take a trip? We can go to the tide pools to hunt for yellow **[1 across]** and pink **[9 across]**. It's okay to look, but we must not **[6 down]**! My favorite thing to do is swim in the **[5 across]**. It feels cool and tastes **[8 down]**. Before you go in, make sure to put on some **[8 across]**. I love to feel the warm, wet **[3 down]** between my toes. We can use it to build a sandcastle. Later on, we can make a big **[7 across]**. We can **[2 down]** hot dogs and marshmallows. Then we can sit around it and tell **[1 down]**. Sounds like a great day at the **[4 down]**!

**Day 69:
Inference**

LUCY'S LASSOS

Help Lucy lasso these problems. Solve the problem on the left. Write the answer in the box.
Then use that number to solve the problem on the right.

1.

$5 \times 2 = \boxed{10}$ $\boxed{10} \times 6 = 60$

2.

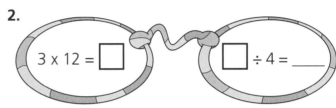

$3 \times 12 = \Box$ $\Box \div 4 = \underline{\hspace{1cm}}$

3.

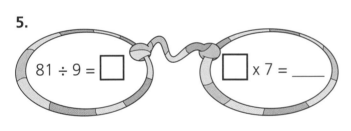

$132 \div 11 = \Box$ $\Box \times 8 = \underline{\hspace{1cm}}$

4.

$4 \times 3 = \Box$ $\Box \times 5 = \underline{\hspace{1cm}}$

5.

$81 \div 9 = \Box$ $\Box \times 7 = \underline{\hspace{1cm}}$

6.

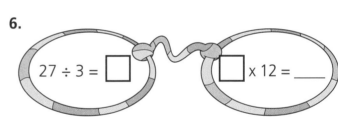

$27 \div 3 = \Box$ $\Box \times 12 = \underline{\hspace{1cm}}$

7.

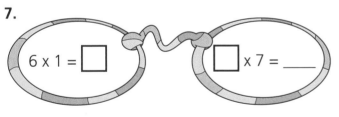

$6 \times 1 = \Box$ $\Box \times 7 = \underline{\hspace{1cm}}$

8.

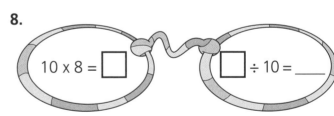

$10 \times 8 = \Box$ $\Box \div 10 = \underline{\hspace{1cm}}$

9.

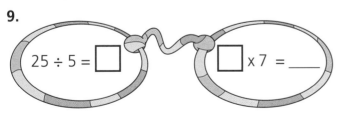

$25 \div 5 = \Box$ $\Box \times 7 = \underline{\hspace{1cm}}$

10.

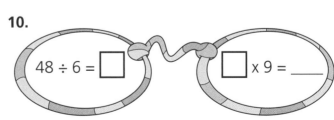

$48 \div 6 = \Box$ $\Box \times 9 = \underline{\hspace{1cm}}$

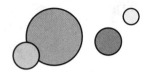
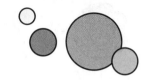

STRANGE PETS

Read the passages. Then answer the questions.

Pot-Bellied Pigs

Some people say that pot-bellied pigs make great pets. They can live right in your home, just like a dog or a cat. But they can also grow to weigh 150 pounds! Pigs are very clean. They can even be trained to use a litter box. Owners claim their pigs are loving, smart, and playful. They also seem to share human feelings. Some owners say their pigs cry! Pot-bellied pigs are very smart. They are easy to train, much like the family dog. Pigs have been trained to play the piano, dance, and even ride a skateboard!

Skunks

Most people stay away from skunks because of their stinky spray. This spray comes from scent glands. To keep a skunk, you must have the scent glands removed. Skunk owners claim these animals are great pets. They say skunks are curious and playful. And they only grow to weigh between 4 and 10 pounds. But skunks can be hard to train. They're very smart but need a lot of attention. Most of all, keep a close eye on this pet. Skunks will steal anything they can get their paws on!

Name four ways these pets are different:

_____

_____

_____

_____

Name four ways these pets are alike:

_____

_____

_____

_____

Which pet would you like to have? Why? Write about it on another piece of paper.

PATTY'S PIZZA PALACE

Read the menu below. Use the menu to solve each problem.

1. Jamie got 2 slices of pizza. The first slice had peppers and tomatoes. The other slice had ham. How much did he spend? _____ $3.25 _____

Pizza, per slice (with cheese)
$1.00
Whole pizza (with cheese)
$6.00

Toppings

Pepperoni 50¢   Peppers 45¢
Tomatoes 30¢   Onions 40¢
Mushrooms 35¢   Olives 25¢
Ham   50¢

2. Maria got one slice of pizza with olives, ham, pepperoni, and tomatoes. She paid with three $1 bills. How much change did she get back?

_____

3. Truc got a whole pizza for her family. It had pepperoni, olives, and mushrooms. How much did she spend? _____

4. Mali and Cris got a whole pizza to share. Mali got onions and mushrooms on her half. Cris got pepperoni and peppers on his half. How much did they spend?

_____

5. Amir got 3 slices of pizza. One slice had ham, one had tomatoes, and one had olives. He paid with a $5 bill. How much change did he get back?

_____

6. Coach Dean got 2 whole pizzas for his baseball team. One pizza had pepperoni and ham. The other pizza had onions and peppers. How much did he spend?

_____

WRITE IT RIGHT

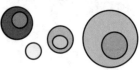

Rewrite each sentence correctly. Add correct punctuation and capital letters where needed.

1. fourth of july is my favorite holiday

_____

2. my brother jorge was born on april 16 2000

_____

3. have you read the book ramona the pest by beverly cleary

_____

4. aunt kathy moved to austin texas

_____

5. teds party was at noon last saturday september 10

_____

6. may i take reggie to play ball at hillside park

_____

7. did mr chase get a bus for our trip to the natural history museum

_____

8. david and his family went to camp black bear over labor day

_____

9. last summer my family visited the grand canyon in arizona

_____

10. mrs chin showed us pictures of blue whales jellyfish and eels

_____

PICK A COMBO

1. You can pick any two toppings you want at Iggy's Ice Cream Shop. The topping choices are: fudge, nuts, caramel, and chocolate chips.

List all of the possible topping combinations.

fudge and

_____

_____

_____

caramel and

_____

nuts and

_____

_____

2. At Candy Castle, you can pick any two candy combos for 50¢. The candy choices are: gummy worms, lemon drops, jellybeans, and mint swirls.

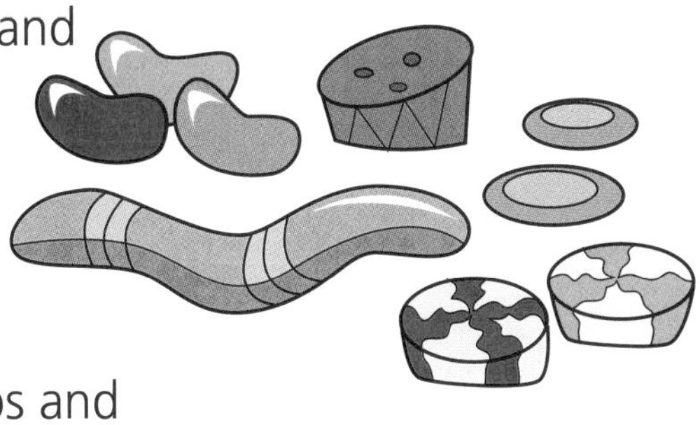

List the candy combinations.

gummy worms and

_____

_____

_____

jellybeans and

_____

lemon drops and

_____

_____

SAME, BUT DIFFERENT

Homophones are words that sound the same but are not spelled the same.
Read each word below. Then write the word that names the picture.
You can see that the words sound the same but are not spelled the same
They are homophones!

1. hair

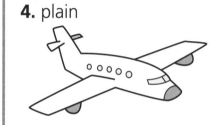

hare

2. ate

3. flour

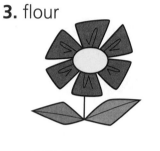

_____

4. plain

_____

5. rode

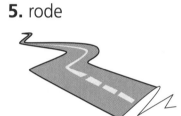

_____

6. sent

_____

7. sale

_____

8. night

_____

9. meet

_____

10. or

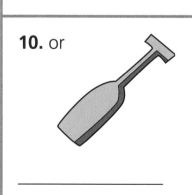

_____

11. weak

SUN MON TUES WED THURS FRI SAT

_____

12. pair

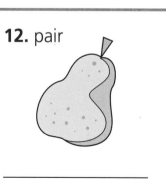

_____

PIZZA FRACTIONS

Write the fractions for the pictures. Then write and solve an addition problem with the fractions.

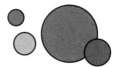

1.

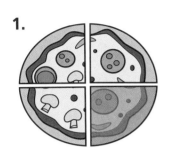

$$\underline{1/4} + \underline{3/4} = \underline{4/4}$$

2.

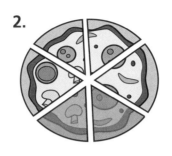

_____ + _____ = _____

3.

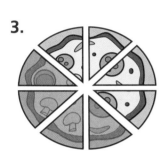

_____ + _____ = _____

4.

_____ + _____ = _____

5.

_____ + _____ = _____

6.

_____ + _____ = _____

PERFECT PARAGRAPH

A **paragraph** begins with a **topic sentence**. This sentence tells what the paragraph is about.
A **paragraph** also has a **main idea** and **supporting details**.

Read the following paragraph. Then go back and underline the topic sentence. Write the main idea and two supporting details below.

The water cycle is the way Earth recycles water. First, the sun warms water. Then the water dries up into the air. Cool air changes the water into vapor as it rises. Then the water vapor changes into water drops. These drops form clouds. The drops get colder. They get heavier and bigger. Finally, the drops are too heavy to stay in the clouds. They fall back to the earth as rain, snow, or hail.

The main idea is: _____
Two supporting details are:

_____

_____

Now, write your own paragraph. You can write about school, a pet, or anything else that interests you. Make sure to include:
- a topic sentence
- a main idea
- supporting details

_____

_____

_____

_____

_____

_____

_____

Use the graph to find the answer to the riddle.
Write the letter that goes with each coordinate on the lines.

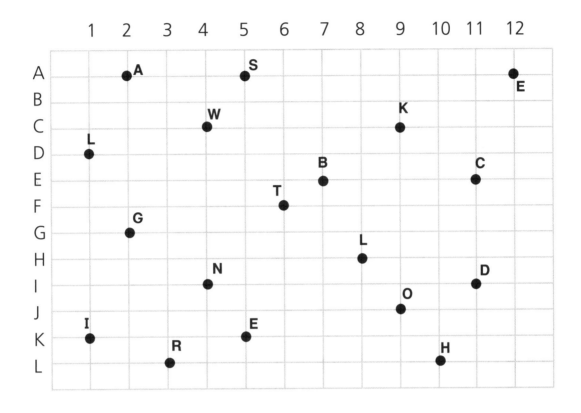

Riddle: Why do cows wear bells?

___ ___ ___ ___ ___   ___ ___ ___ ___ ___
(F,6) (L,10) (A,12) (K,1) (L,3)   (L,10) (J,9) (L,3) (I,4) (A,5)

___ ___ ___ , ___   ___ ___ ___ ___
(I,11) (J,9) (I,4) (F,6)   (C,4) (J,9) (L,3) (C,9)

MIMI'S MARVELOUS MUFFINS

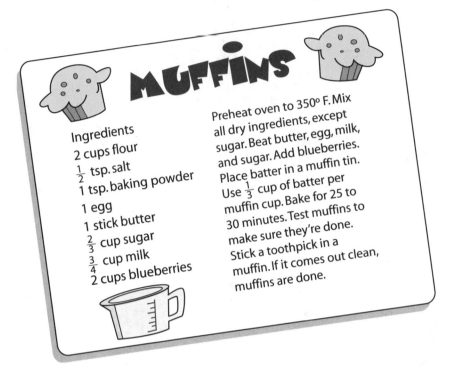

Ingredients
2 cups flour
$\frac{1}{2}$ tsp. salt
1 tsp. baking powder
1 egg
1 stick butter
$\frac{2}{3}$ cup sugar
$\frac{3}{4}$ cup milk
2 cups blueberries

Preheat oven to 350° F. Mix all dry ingredients, except sugar. Beat butter, egg, milk, and sugar. Add blueberries. Place batter in a muffin tin. Use $\frac{1}{3}$ cup of batter per muffin cup. Bake for 25 to 30 minutes. Test muffins to make sure they're done. Stick a toothpick in a muffin. If it comes out clean, muffins are done.

1. This recipe gives directions for making:
a) cake
b) muffins
c) cookies

2. Which of these items is not needed to make this recipe?
a) spoon
b) bowl
c) baking sheet

3. Which ingredient is added last to this recipe?
a) sugar
b) blueberries
c) egg

4. What is the first step in this recipe?
a) Mix together all dry ingredients.
b) Preheat oven to 350° F.
c) Test muffins to make sure they're done.

5. What might be the next step in this recipe?
a) Let muffins cool.
b) Eat muffins.
c) Put away ingredients.

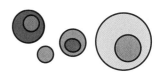

NUMBER LINES

Look at each number line. It shows a pattern.
Complete the pattern by writing the numbers over the dots on the number line.

0 1 2 3 4

1.   0   3   6   9   **12 15 18**

2.   4   6   8   10

3.   0   4   8   12

4.   8   9   10   9   8

5.   5   10   15   20

6.   30 26 22 18

7.   0   10   20   30

8.   1   2   4   8

UNDERSTANDING POETRY

Read the passage. It is part of a poem called "The Walrus and the Carpenter" by Lewis Carroll.
Then answer the questions.

The sun was shining on the sea,
Shining with all his might:
He did his very best to make
The billows smooth and bright—
And this was odd, because it was
The middle of the night.

The moon was shining sulkily,
Because she thought the sun
Had no business to be there
After the day was done—
"It's very rude of him," she said,
"To come and spoil the fun!"

The sea was wet as wet could be,
The sands were dry as dry.
You could not see a cloud, because
No cloud was in the sky;
No birds were flying overhead—
There were no birds to fly.

1. What two objects act like people?

_____

3. Why could you not see a cloud?

_____

_____

5. Which two adjectives are repeated in the last verse?

_____

_____

2. Why was it odd for the sun to be shining?

_____

_____

4. Write the three rhyming words from the first verse:

_____

_____

 # MIX OF MEASURES

Read each problem. Then circle your answer.

1. Nina needed new carpet. She measured her bedroom using:

a) yards
b) inches
c) miles

2. It was a hot summer day. The thermometer showed:

a) 32° F
b) 62° F
c) 85° F

3. Tom weighed a bag of apples in the store. He put them on a:

a) measuring cup
b) scale
c) ruler

4. The vet weighed Annie's hamster. He weighed the hamster using:

a) pounds
b) feet
c) ounces

5. Dad took us for a ride in his new car. When we got home, he said we drove 35:

a) yards
b) miles
c) inches

6. Tad put on his winter coat and gloves. The thermometer showed:

a) 90° F
b) 75° F
c) 2° F

7. Katie drew a picture in her notebook. She measured it for a frame using:

a) inches
b) feet
c) ounces

8. Mom needed $\frac{1}{2}$ cup of milk for the cake batter. She measured the milk using:

a) inches
b) ounces
c) pounds

9. Gabe added a little bit of salt to his soup. He used a:

a) teaspoon
b) cup
c) ruler

WHERE DO I FIND IT?

Do you know how to find information? It can help you when you are reading or writing.
Circle the correct reference for each question.

1. To find the week's sports scores, you should look in the:
a) dictionary
b) encyclopedia
c) newspaper

2. To find out where Japan is, you should look in the:
a) atlas
b) thesaurus
c) phone book

3. To find the page number for a chapter, you should look in the:
a) dictionary
b) newspaper
c) table of contents

4. To find the meaning of the word *timid*, you should look in the:
a) atlas
b) dictionary
c) encyclopedia

5. To find topics in a book, you should look in the:
a) index
b) thesaurus
c) title page

6. To find a synonym for the word *happy*, you should look in the:
a) thesaurus
b) dictionary
c) atlas

7. To find out about today's weather, you should look in the:
a) table of contents
b) phone book
c) newspaper

8. To research the history of ballet, you should look in the:
a) encyclopedia
b) dictionary
c) index

WHAT ARE THE ODDS?

Predicting is an important math skill. It can help you come close to an answer without actually solving a problem. Read each problem carefully. Then circle the best answer.

1. You flip a quarter 10 times. About how many times will it be tails?

a) 2 in 10
b) 5 in 10
c) 10 in 10

2. A jar contains 100 jellybeans. 60 are red, 20 are green and 20 are purple. You take 1 jellybean. What is the chance you will pick a green jellybean?

a) 6 in 10
b) 2 in 10
c) all the same

3. A bag contains 40 marbles. 16 are blue. You take one marble. What is the chance you will get a blue marble?

a) 8 in 20
b) 10 in 20
c) 2 in 20

4. You have 16 pairs of socks. 3 pairs are black, 8 pairs are white, 5 pairs are brown. What is the chance you will grab a pair of white socks?

a) 1 in 4
b) 1 in 3
c) 1 in 2

5. There are 12 ladybugs in the jar. 4 are red, 6 are orange, 2 are white. If you open the lid, what is the chance that a white bug will fly out?

a) 6 in 12
b) 1 in 6
c) 1 in 4

6. You throw a 5 for your first roll of the die. What is the chance you will throw a 5 on your next roll?

a) 1 in 5
b) 2 in 5
c) 1 in 6

MATCHING MEANINGS

Some words have several meanings.

Choose the sentence that has the same meaning as the underlined word in the first sentence. Circle the letter.

1. Mom held Brie's <u>hand</u> when they crossed the street.
a) I cut my <u>hand</u> on the fence.
b) Please <u>hand</u> me the apple.
c) The crowd gave her a <u>hand</u> for her speech.

2. Did you go to the county <u>fair</u>?
a) My teacher is <u>fair</u> when it comes to grades.
b) The princess was known as <u>fair</u> and sweet.
c) Mom won first prize for her pie at the <u>fair</u>.

3. Make sure to <u>check</u> your answers.
a) Did you <u>check</u> whether the baby is asleep?
b) Place a <u>check</u> next to each item you want.
c) Dad wrote a <u>check</u> for my new bike.

4. Enzo's last name is hard to <u>spell</u>.
a) Grandma laid down for a <u>spell</u>.
b) How do you <u>spell</u> the word *tomorrow*?
c) The fairy cast a magic <u>spell</u> over the prince.

5. My <u>back</u> is sore from carrying those boxes.
a) Manny will <u>back</u> the car out of the garage.
b) Jenny just got <u>back</u> from her trip.
c) Bill felt the ball hit him in the <u>back</u>.

6. Kara got a new <u>lock</u> for her bike.
a) Did you <u>lock</u> the back door?
b) The <u>lock</u> on the gate was easy to open.
c) Mom cut a <u>lock</u> of the baby's hair.

7. I added two eggs to the cake <u>batter</u>.
a) Brownie <u>batter</u> is thick and sweet.
b) Branches will <u>batter</u> the window in a storm.
c) Steph is the best <u>batter</u> on our softball team.

8. A big <u>wave</u> crashed on the beach.
a) I will <u>wave</u> to Joey on stage.
b) Lin has a curly <u>wave</u> in her long hair.
c) Can you surf on that big <u>wave</u>?

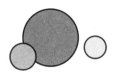
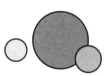

Read the clues to find the secret number.

1. It is an odd number.

It is in the triangle and the square.

It is more than 6.

It is divisible by 3.

The secret number is: _____

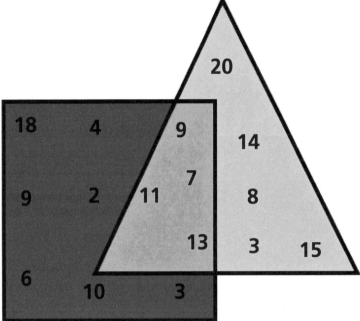

2. It is not an odd number.

It is in the circle.

It is less than 16.

It is divisible by 5.

The secret number is: _____

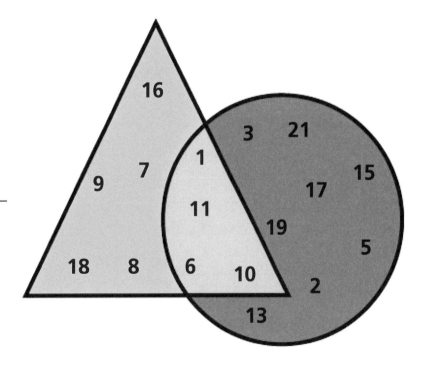

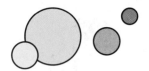
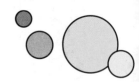

HOWL IN THE WILD

Read the passage below. Then answer the questions.

Have you ever heard a wolf howl? It is a spooky sound. It is a lonely sound. Wolves make many kinds of sounds. They bark, woof, whine, and yelp. They also moan and growl. But when we think of wolves, we think of howling. Why do wolves howl?

The center of a wolf's life is its pack. Howling is the glue that keeps the pack together. You could say that the pack that howls together, stays together! Wolves wander over large areas to find food. They are often separated from each other. Of all their calls, howling is the only one that works over great distances. If you separate a wolf from its pack, it will soon begin howling over and over again.

There are two main reasons that wolves howl. They howl to keep the pack together. They also howl to keep enemies away. The enemies are usually other wolf packs. Wolves don't really howl at the moon. They howl to talk to each other.

1. Name three sounds wolves make, besides howls.

_____

2. What does a wolf howl sound like?

_____

3. What is the center of a wolf's life?

_____

4. Why might a wolf be away from its pack?

_____

5. What are the two main reasons wolves howl?

_____

_____

BASEBALL SEASON

Read about the baseball stadium. Then solve the problems.

The baseball stadium has 4,500 seats. There are:
- 700 seats in Section A
- 1,800 seats in Section B
- 1,200 seats in Section C
- 800 seats in Section D

1. These seats were sold for the first game:
- 550 seats in Section A
- 1,200 seats in Section B
- 800 seats in Section C
- 730 seats in Section D

How many seats were left over? _____

2. Section A seats are twice the cost of Section B seats. Section C seats are $5 less than Section B seats. Section D seats are half the cost of Section C seats. Section B seats are $12.00. How much are seats in:

Section A? _____ Section B? _____ Section C? _____ Section D? _____

3. The stadium completely sold out for $\frac{1}{4}$ of the games this season. There are 12 games in a season. How many seats were sold out this season? _____

4. Half of the seats in each section were sold by Friday. On Saturday, these seats were sold:
- 50 in Section A
- 85 in Section B
- 250 in Section C
- 100 in Section D

a. How many seats were sold on Friday? _____

b. How many seats were sold on Saturday? _____

c. How many seats were sold all together? _____

When you read, knowing who, what, when, and where helps you understand what is happening in a story. Write **who**, **what**, **when**, or **where** for each phrase below.

1. in the forest _____*where*_____

2. my brother and I _____

3. a hungry bear_____

4. after sunset _____

5. ten colorful butterflies _____

6. a helpful forest ranger _____

7. over the mountain _____

8. early in the morning _____

9. at the same time _____

10. friendly campers _____

11. in the cool lake _____

12. the steep trail _____

13. inside the tent _____

14. a crackling campfire _____

15. after the thunderstorm _____

16. up the pine tree _____

17. his best friend _____

18. a newborn fawn _____

19. around the meadow _____

20. over the cliff _____

SWITCH IT

Finish each multiplication sentence.

1. If 7 x 5 = 35 . . .   then 5 x ☐ 7 = 35.

2. If 3 x 12 = 36 . . .   then ☐ x 3 = 36.

3. If 5 x 4 = 20 . . .   then ☐ x 5 = 20.

4. If 11 x 6 = 66 . . .   then 6 x ☐ = 66.

5. If 8 x 3 = 24 . . .   then 3 x 8 = ☐ .

6. If 6 x 7 = 42 . . .   then 7 x 6 = ☐ .

7. If 9 x 5 = 45 . . .   then ☐ x 9 = 45.

8. If 8 x 10 = 80 . . .   then 10 x ☐ = 80.

9. If 12 x 11 = 132 . . .   then 11 x ☐ = 132.

10. If 9 x 6 = 54 . . .   then ☐ x 9 = 54.

11. If 2 x 5 = 10 . . .   then 5 x 2 = ☐ .

12. If 4 x 12 = 48 . . .   then 12 x ☐ = 48.

ANSWER KEY

Page 4
Nouns are placed in the story in this order:
ant, stream, leaf, tree, dove, stick, hunter, foot, woods, heart.

Page 5

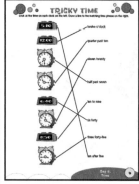

10, 20, 30, 40, 50, 60, 70, 80, 90, 100

Page 6
Tiny and *huge* are the same color.
Smooth and *rough* are the same color.
Strong and *weak* are the same color.
True and *false* are the same color.
High and *low* are the same color.
Right and *wrong* are the same color.

Page 7
2. 20
3. 18
4. 15
5. 12
6. 21
7. 22
8. 13
9. 12
10. 14

Page 8
2. ten, huge, colorful; 3
3. one, striped; 2
4. tall, brown, green; 3
5. yellow; 1
6. small, furry; 2
7. sour, bad; 2
8. sweet, little, funny; 3
9. best; 1
10. red, yellow; 2

Page 9

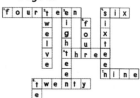

Page 10
1. 5, 4, 2, 1, 3
2. 1, 3, 5, 4, 2
3. 5, 1, 3, 4, 2

Page 11
2. 25¢, 25¢, 25¢, 10¢, 10¢
3. 10¢, 5¢, 5¢, 5¢, 1¢
4. 25¢, 25¢, 25¢, 5¢

Page 12
2. bite
3. track
4. rust
5. thing
6. street
7. drop
8. brake
9. floor
10. moon

Page 13
1. Two bugs are colored.
2. Five bugs are colored.
3. Six bugs are colored.
4. Six bugs are colored.
5. One bug is colored.
6. Six bugs are colored.

Page 14

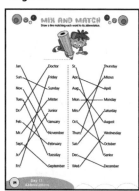

Page 15
2. 15 – 7 = 8
3. 15 – 10 = 5

4. 15 – 3 = 12
5. 15 – 6 = 9
6. 15 – 8 = 7
7. 15 – 5 = 10
8. 15 – 9 = 6

Page 16
Happy and *glad* are the same color.
Yell and *shout* are the same color.
Jump and *leap* are the same color.
Quiet and *silent* are the same color.
Noisy and *loud* are the same color.
Smile and *grin* are the same color.

Page 17

Page 18
Circle:
1. today
2. stain
3. played
4. away
5. whale
6. waist
7. chain
8. snake
9. train
10. brain

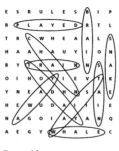

Page 19
1. less
2. more
3. less
4. less

5. more
6. more
7. less
8. less
9. more
10. less
11. less
12. more
13. more
14. less
15. less
16. more

Page 20
2. Tigers, Trains, Trees, Turkey
3. Magnets, Mice, Money, Moose
4. Baseball, Bats, Bees, Boating
5. Hats, History, Holidays, Horses
6. Cars, Chairs, China, Clowns
7. School, Soccer, Spain, Stars
8. Whales, Wigs, Wind, Wishing
9. Rhinos, Rice, Roads, Rockets

Page 21
2. ounces
3. ounces
4. pounds
5. ounces
6. pounds
7. ounces
8. pounds
9. ounces

Page 22
1. Spiders are arachnids.
2. Spiders eat insects.
3. Baby spiders are called spiderlings.
4. They help people by eating bad insects.

Page 23
2. 22, 33
3. 65, 19
4. 17, 51
5. 13, 14
6. 46, 50
7. 16, 28
8. 62, 13
9. 33, 19

Page 24

Page 25
1. 9
2. 24
3. 12
4. 8
5. 20
6. 5

Page 26
2. doorknob
3. seashell
4. keyboard
5. barefoot
6. postcard
7. shoelace
8. peanut
9. pancake
10. sunshine
Answer: snake shake

Page 27

Page 28
2. bakes, baked
3. bark, barked
4. gallop, galloped
5. move, moved
6. want, wanted
7. talk, talked
8. visit, visited
9. melts, melted
10. crawl, crawled

Page 29

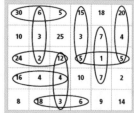

Page 30
Circle:
home
boat
clock
snow
smoke
soap
throw
rock
drove
roast
2. roast
3. throw
4. snow
5. clock
6. drove
7. soap
8. boat
9. smoke
10. rock

Page 31
2. 18 units, $4\frac{1}{2}$ inches
3. 24 units, 6 inches
4. 10 units, $2\frac{1}{2}$ inches
5. 20 units, 5 inches
6. 14 units, $3\frac{1}{2}$ inches

Page 32
2. We'll
3. didn't
4. I'm
5. aren't
6. don't
7. haven't
8. isn't
9. Here's
10. I'll

Page 33
2. 4 weeks
3. 120 minutes
4. 1 day
5. 14 hours
6. 56 days
7. 6 months
8. 2 hours

Page 34
Circle:
1. ice
2. lime
3. tie
4. this
5. stir
6. little
7. tiny
8. spider
9. circle
10. drive

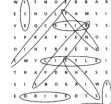

Page 35

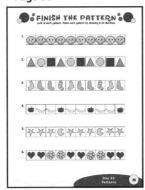

Page 36
1. Meg's new shoes are red.
2. Meg plays softball.
3. She knew her shoes were special right away.
4. On Meg's way home, she flew.
5. Answers will vary.

Page 37

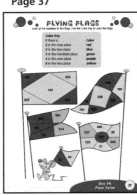

Page 38
Poems will vary.

Page 39
2. no
3. yes
4. no
5. yes
6. no

Page 40
2. zebras
3. foxes
4. friends
5. snakes
6. bunches
7. rocks
8. bunnies
9. bushes
10. babies

Page 41
2. chocolate
3. five
4. four
5. 32 people
6. Answers will vary.

Page 42
2. knows; knew
3. breaks; broke
4. feels; felt
5. swings; swung
6. sink; sank
7. makes; made
8. throws; threw
9. feeds; fed
10. draws; drew

Page 43
1. $\frac{3}{6}$
2. $\frac{1}{3}$
3. $\frac{2}{8}$
4. $\frac{1}{4}$
5. $\frac{5}{10}$
6. $\frac{3}{3}$
7. $\frac{5}{6}$
8. $\frac{4}{4}$
9. $\frac{8}{9}$

Page 44
Circle:
spell
wheel
peach
dear
three
street
clean
dead
eel
went
2. went
3. peach
4. dead
5. street
6. eel
7. three
8. dear
9. wheel
10. clean

Page 45
2. 40¢; forty
3. 55¢; fifty-five
4. 31¢; thirty-one
5. 64¢; sixty-four
6. 86¢; forty-two
8. 90¢; ninety
Answer: Jefferson

Page 46
1. Circle: First, tiny seedlings. Azra knew that soon pink and purple. Soon, big flowers!
2. Circle: Are Asian and African. Have five front toes. Like elephants?
3. Circle: Got a snowboard for his birthday. Over the snow really fast! Rides better and better.
4. Circle: All the planets. Trip to the moon. To my family.
5. Answers will vary, but all sentences should be complete.

Page 47

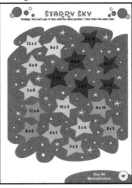

Page 48
2. A; hiking
3. B; baseball
4. F; boating
5. E; biking

Page 49
2. Train 10
3. 2 hours and 45 minutes
4. 30 minutes
5. 2 hours
6. 2:00 PM

Page 50
2. Wow, there are many, many stars in the sky! E
3. Nine planets are in our solar system. T
4. Would you like to go to the moon? A
5. Bring moon rocks back from your trip. C
6. Get ready to ride the fast rocket. C
7. Mars is called the red planet. T
8. Is the sun a planet or a star? A
9. Never look at the sun. C
10. How many rings are around Saturn? A

Page 51
Estimates and measurements will vary.

Page 52
1. a; Fall is a great season.
2. c; You can train your cat.
3. b; The circus is fun.
4. a; Bike safety is important.

Page 53
Answer: HE QUACKS UP
Answer: ROAD HOG

Page 54
Circle:
1. turtle
2. cube
3. burst
4. push
5. pupil
6. true
7. fur
8. funny
9. fuel
10. blue

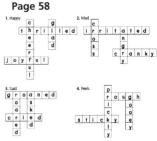

Page 55
2. 4; 12; 24; 32
3. 18; 30; 54; 66
4. 16; 40; 80; 96
5. 20; 40; 90; 120

Page 56
Answers will vary.

Page 57
1. 8,295 = 8,000 + 200 + 90 + 5
2. 1,047 = 1,000 + 0 + 40 + 7
3. 9,962 = 9,000 + 900 + 60 + 2
4. 6,813 = 6,000 + 800 + 10 + 3
5. 359, 395, 539, 593, 935, 953
Circle: 359
Cross out: 953
6. 268, 286, 628, 682, 826, 862
Circle: 268
Cross out: 862

Page 58

1. Happy: thrilled, eager, glad, joyful
2. Mad: irritated, cross, angry, cranky
3. Said: groaned, asked, cried, added
4. Feels: proud, nice, lovely, sticky, rough

Page 59
1. 35
2. 25
3. 25
4. 10
5. 75
6. 100

Page 60
Answers will vary.

Letters will vary.

1. 8 in.   2. 20 in.
3. 14 in.   4. 10 cm.
5. 24 in.   6. 18 cm.

1. Underline: I sat by the window so I could watch the world go by. We crossed over a river. When we passed through the train stations, people waved at me! I waved back with a big smile on my face.
2. Underline: It can be rain. It can be spray from a garden hose. It can come from a water fountain.
3. Answers will vary.

2. Keri 4, Ana 1, Ahmad 2, Juan 3
3. 48 coins

Articles will vary.

A yardstick

2. bicycle
3. unhappy
4. underground
5. overpaid
6. unable
7. multicolored
8. miscount
9. nonstop
10. reheat
New words will vary.
Sentences will vary.

1. c
2. d
3. a
4. c
5. b
6. b
7. Answers will vary.

2. biggest
3. longer
4. tallest

5. stronger
6. faster
7. brighter
8. funniest
9. harder
10. shortest
11. and 12. Sentences will vary.

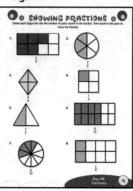

2. 3 x 12 = 36;
36 ÷ 4 = 9
3. 132 ÷ 11 = 12;
12 x 8 = 96
4. 4 x 3 = 12;
12 x 5 = 60
5. 81 ÷ 9 = 9;
9 x 7 = 63
6. 27 ÷ 3 = 9;
9 x 12 = 108
7. 6 x 1 = 6;
6 x 7 = 42
8. 10 x 8 = 80;
80 ÷ 10 = 8
9. 25 ÷ 5 = 5;
5 x 7 = 35
10. 48 ÷ 6 = 8;
8 x 9 = 72

Four ways these pets are different:
Pigs weigh more than skunks.
Pigs are easier to train than skunks.
Pigs have human-like feelings.
Skunks steal.
Skunks have scent glands.
Four ways these pets are alike:
Both have four legs.
Both make great pets.
Both are smart.
Both are playful.

1. $3.25
2. 45¢
3. $7.10
4. $7.70
5. 95¢
6. $13.85

1. Fourth of July is my favorite holiday.
2. My brother Jorge was born on April 16, 2000.
3. Have you read the book Ramona the Pest, by Beverly Cleary?
4. Aunt Kathy moved to Austin, Texas.
5. Ted's party was at noon last Saturday, September 10.
6. May I take Reggie to play ball at Hillside Park?
7. Did Mr. Chase get a bus for our trip to the Natural History Museum?
8. David and his family went to Camp Black Bear over Labor Day.
9. Last summer my family visited the Grand Canyon in Arizona.
10. Mrs. Chin showed us pictures of blue whales, jellyfish, and eels.

1. fudge and nuts, fudge and caramel, fudge and chocolate chips
nuts and caramel, nuts and chocolate chips
caramel and chocolate chips
2. gummy worms and lemon drops, gummy worms and jellybeans, gummy worms and mint swirls
lemon drops and jellybeans, lemon drops and mint swirls
jellybeans and mint swirls

2. eight
3. flower
4. plane
5. road

6. cent
7. sail
8. knight
9. meat
10. oar
11. week
12. pear

2. $\frac{2}{6} + \frac{2}{6} = \frac{4}{6}$
3. $\frac{4}{8} + \frac{3}{8} = \frac{7}{8}$
4. $\frac{5}{10} + \frac{2}{10} = \frac{7}{10}$
5. $\frac{1}{5} + \frac{4}{5} = \frac{5}{5}$
6. $\frac{3}{5} + \frac{2}{5} = \frac{5}{5}$

Topic sentence: The water cycle is the way Earth recycles water.
The main idea is: The water cycle recycles water.
Two supporting details: Details will vary, but should include any two sentences after the topic sentence. Paragraphs will vary.

Their horns don't work.

1. b   2. c
3. b   4. b
5. a

2. 4, 6, 8, 10, 12, 14, 16
3. 0, 4, 8, 12, 16, 20, 24
4. 8, 9, 10, 9, 8, 7, 6, 5, 4
5. 5, 10, 15, 20, 25, 30, 35, 40
6. 30, 26, 22, 18, 14, 10, 6, 2
7. 0, 10, 20, 30, 40, 50, 60, 70
8. 1, 2, 4, 8, 16, 32, 64

1. The sun and the moon.
2. It was the middle of the night.
3. No cloud was in the sky.
4. might, bright, night
5. wet, dry

1. a   2. c   3. b
4. c   5. b   6. c
7. a   8. b   9. a

1. c   2. a
3. c   4. b
5. a   6. a
7. c   8. a

1. b   2. b
3. a   4. c

5. b   6. c

1. a   2. c
3. a   4. b
5. c   6. b
7. a   8. c

1. The secret number is 9.
2. The secret number is 10.

1. Any three: bark, woof, whine, yelp, moan, growl
2. A wolf's howl sounds spooky and lonely.
3. The center of a wolf's life is its pack.
4. A wolf might be away from its pack to find food.
5. Wolves howl to keep the pack together and to keep enemies away.

1. 1,220 seats
2. Section A: $24; Section B: $12; Section C: $7; Section D: $3.50
3. 13,500 seats
4. a. 2,250 seats
   b. 485 seats
   c. 2,735 seats

2. who
3. what
4. when
5. what
6. who
7. where
8. when
9. when
10. who
11. where
12. what
13. where
14. what
15. when
16. where
17. who
18. what
19. where
20. where

2. 12
3. 4
4. 11
5. 24
6. 42
7. 5
8. 8
9. 12
10. 6
11. 10
12. 4